I0424677

This book belongs to

____

By
SKIPPY

www.ingramcontent.com/pod-product-compliance
Lightning Source LLC
Chambersburg PA
CBHW020326290526
45785CB00007B/2929
9781077611566